AF848667

Great Mysteries

UFOs

by Janet Riehecky
illustrated by Dan Siculan

Created by THE CHILD'S WORLD

Distributed by CHILDRENS PRESS®
Chicago, Illinois

cover photograph courtesy of Major Ret. Colman S. VonKeviczky, MMSE; ICUFON
cover design by Kathryn Schoenick

CHILDRENS PRESS HARDCOVER EDITION
ISBN 0-516-06218-2

CHILDRENS PRESS PAPERBACK EDITION
ISBN 0-516-46218-0

Library of Congress Cataloging-in-Publication Data

Riehecky, Janet, 1953-
UFOs / by Janet Riehecky ; illustrated by Dan Siculan.
p. cm. — (Great mysteries)
Includes index.
Summary: Traces the history of UFO sightings and describes the general characteristics and official explanations of encounters with unidentified flying objects.
ISBN 0-89565-453-9
1. Unidentified flying objects—Juvenile literature. [1. Unidentified flying objects.] I. Siculan, Dan, ill. II. Title. III. Series: Great mysteries (Elgin, Ill.)
TL789.R53 1989
001.9'42—dc19 88-25730
CIP
AC

©1989 The Child's World, Inc.
Elgin, IL
All rights reserved. Printed in U.S.A.

1 2 3 4 5 6 7 8 9 10 11 12 R 97 96 95 94 93 92 91 90 89

Great Mysteries

UFOs

Appreciation is expressed to George M. Eberhart and Mark Rodeghier of the J. Allen Hynek Center for UFO Studies (CUFOS) for their critique of this manuscript and their generously offered assistance.

CONTENTS

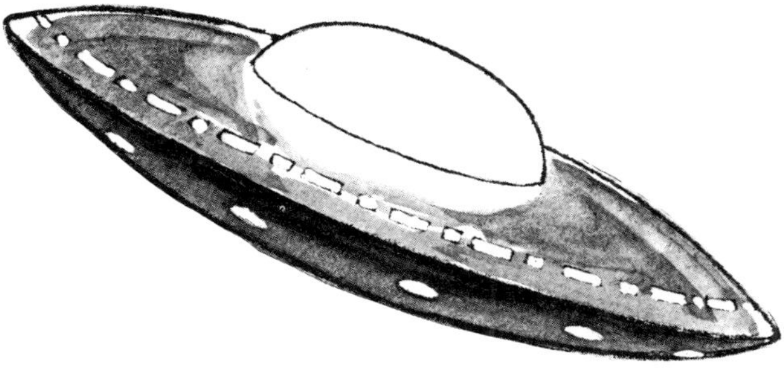

Chapter 1

Is Seeing Believing?

Have you ever seen something in the sky you couldn't explain? Maybe you saw strange lights. Maybe you saw a weird shape. Later you found out that the lights were from an airplane or meteor. The shape was just a kite caught in a tree. You laughed and forgot about it. Sometimes, though, people see things that can't be explained. Scientists call anything that is seen in the sky that can't be explained an Unidentified Flying Object or UFO.

UFOs in History

Lots of UFOs have been reported—in fact, people have been seeing them for over two thousand years. Some of the reports are just wild tales, but others are very believable.

A famous scholar named Gregory of Tours, who lived fourteen hundred years ago, reported seeing several UFOs near the city of Tours, which is in present-day France. In his book, *History of the Franks,* he writes that one year three or four "great, shining places" appeared frequently in the sky. They were so large and bright, some people thought they were new suns. Eventually, they disappeared, but they were never explained.

Several years later a single light suddenly appeared in the sky. Gregory wrote that it sparkled in a great blackness in the sky and then shot a ray of light to the earth, "like smoke from a fire." One Easter, Gregory and many others saw two "great fires" in the sky. They hovered in the sky for two hours, then came together in a great flame and vanished.

These descriptions are familiar to anyone who reads UFO reports today. Huge lights hovering in the sky, mysterious rays, and lights joining and then vanishing are described in many reports. And Gregory's history is not the only history to describe such unexplainable sights in the sky. Other accounts also describe incidents similar to sightings occuring today.

A thousand years ago in a village called Lyons, in France, a mob of people saw an "airship" in the sky. Then they saw three men and a woman get off the airship. The mob became scared and wanted to burn the people. The men and woman who had been on the airship tried to tell the mob that there was nothing to be afraid of. They tried to describe some of the things they had learned from the "miraculous men" on the airship.

Then the Archbishop heard the noise. He came out of his house. He stopped the mob from attacking the four people and scolded the villagers. "It is impossible for people to come out of the sky. These people could not possibly have been on a ship in the air. I don't care what you think you saw!" And he sent everyone home.

Today, too, people in authority often dismiss reports of UFOs with a simple, "There can't be such things as UFOs." They insist people can't have seen what they say they've seen and can't have done what they say they've done.

Explanations

Authorities have always tried to provide explanations for UFO sightings. Often these explanations made a lot of sense. But by the 1950's, authorities wanted to explain UFOs so badly, some of the explanations became stranger than the idea of UFOs itself. Authorities tried to convince people all they'd seen were clouds, even if there weren't any that day. They told trained pilots that the pilots had not been able to recognize weather balloons. Radar blips that seemed to indicate the presence of UFOs were explained away as "just echoes of natural objects." Silvery disks that looked like man-made crafts were said to be light from the planet Venus. And if all else failed, sightings were dismissed as "swamp gas."

People who report UFO sightings resent these kinds of explanations. They want to be taken seriously, not treated as if they are sick or crazy. They are often just ordinary people who are going about ordinary business when

"Don't worry about it, dear. It's probably just swamp gas."

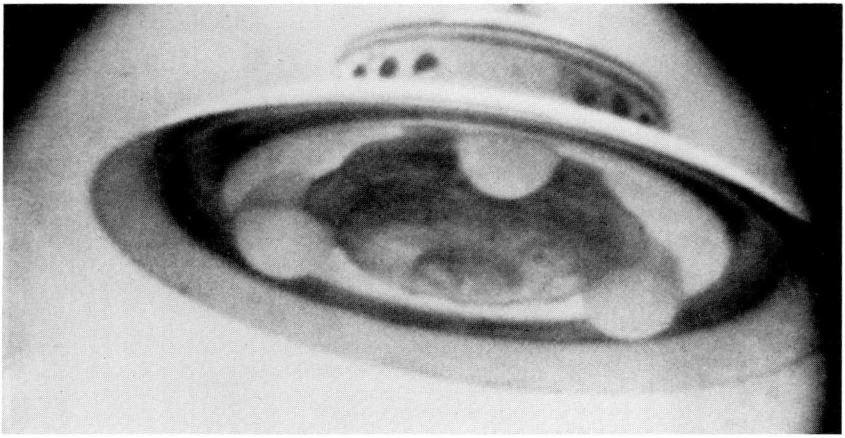
Adamski's "spaceship from Venus" (courtesy of Major Ret. Colman S. Vonkeviczky, MMSE, ICUFON)

something strange happens. Maybe it wasn't alien spacecraft that they saw, but they did see something unusual.

Kooks

One reason many people do not take UFO sightings seriously is that some people who have reported them have made some really crazy claims. For instance, in 1953 a man named George Adamski claimed that creatures from Venus had chosen him to be their ambassador.

Adamski, who died in 1965, traveled the world telling stories about his meetings with the Venusians. He said he took trips with them on their flying saucers. He told of having been to cities on the dark side of the moon. When early Russian photographs of the dark side of the moon did not show any cities, he claimed the Russians retouched the photographs to mislead the United States.

None of Adamski's predictions or descriptions have ever been confirmed by scientists. But there were (and are) many people who believe him anyway. Most people, though, just say that he proves that people who believe in UFOs are kooks.

Hoaxes

Another reason some people do not take UFOs seriously is that some sightings are deliberately faked. One famous incident happened in 1967. Two teenage boys, Dan and Grant Jaroslaw, sent three photographs to a newspaper. These photos showed a "flying saucer" over their

The Jaroslaw photograph (courtesy of Wide World Photos)

Lake St. Clair, Michigan, home. Air Force personnel investigated and said they couldn't explain the pictures. They believed the photos were real, even though neither of the boys passed a lie-detector test. Ten years later the boys confessed that they'd hung a small model from a thread and taken the pictures.

UFOs

Perhaps 5% of UFO reports are deliberate hoaxes. And as many as 85% are mistakes of one kind or another. That accounts for nine out of ten UFO sightings. But that still leaves thousands of recorded sightings that the experts cannot explain. These sightings are not hoaxes, are not imagination, and are not swamp gas. These sightings are truly "unidentified," and they are the subject of this book.

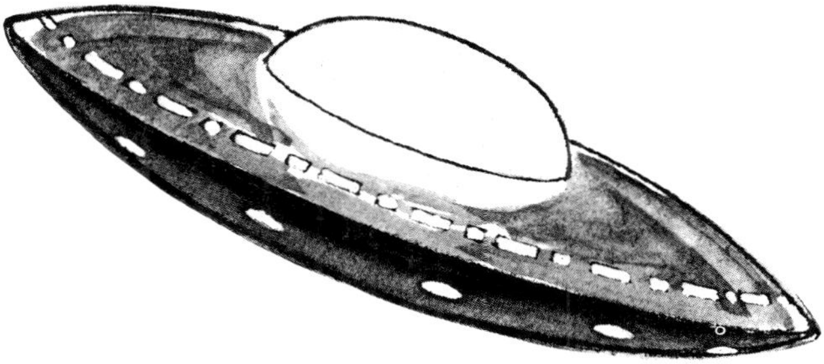

Chapter 2

What is a UFO?

On June 24, 1947, Kenneth Arnold, an experienced pilot, was flying near Mount Rainier, Washington. It was about three o'clock in the afternoon. He saw nine disk-shaped objects flying together in an organized pattern. They were like no aircraft he had ever seen.

As the objects passed various spots on the mountain range, Arnold tried to figure out how fast they were going. The answer both surprised and scared him. It was fifty miles between Mount Rainer and Mount Adams. The objects covered that distance in one minute and forty-two seconds! That meant they were going faster than 1600 miles per hour—and no aircraft Arnold knew of in 1947 could travel that fast.

Arnold was afraid that what he saw might be some enemy's secret weapons, so he reported his sighting.

When he tried to describe the objects, he said they moved, "like saucers would if you skipped them across the water." A Portland, Oregon, newspaper reporter picked up the phrase, and soon "flying saucers" became a popular name for something more and more people were starting to see.

For suddenly UFOs were everywhere. Before the 1940's there was an occasional sighting. Since then, thousands of reports have come in from all over the world. For almost fifty years now, UFOs have been sighted daily. But what is it that people are seeing?

UFO Characteristics

Lights

Well, most of the time people see lights—strange lights. UFOs often light up the night, shining more brightly than the stars or moon or other familiar lights. People report all different colors of lights on UFOs, though most often they report red or white lights. Sometimes the lights are arranged in unusual patterns such as circles. Often they "pulsate," that is, they dim and then grow brighter in a regular pattern. Many reports say that the lights actually change colors as the UFOs move through the sky.

Movement

And wow—do they move! UFOs are reported to move in ways no aircraft we know of can move. Radar has tracked them going over 9000 miles per hour, and pilots report observing them move even faster than that. Yet

Unidentified lights over Montreal, 1973 (courtesy of Major Ret. Colman S. Vonkeviczky, MMSE, ICUFON)

UFOs can often stop almost instantly without any gradual slowdown. They turn abruptly right or left, without losing speed. Sometimes they stop and stay still, or hover, for minutes. Then they take off at incredible speeds. They have been reported to chase cars and even to split apart in the air and then rejoin. And they do this without making a sound.

Sound

The faster our known aircraft go, the more noise they make. Yet UFOs go faster than some of our rockets and rarely make any noise at all. About 10% to 15% of witnesses do report hearing a buzzing or humming sound, but the rest of the time witnesses report hearing nothing at all—from objects they estimate are only a few hundred feet away.

Locations

UFOs appear more often in some kinds of places than in others. In Exeter, New Hampshire, many sightings occurred over a period of several weeks. Most were near various electrical power lines. Investigators in other areas have also noticed this "preference" for power sources. And UFOs have been noticed more frequently near swampy areas, bodies of fresh water, and military installations.

Effects on Surroundings

Sometimes UFOs don't just fly past, leaving no trace of their passage. People report all kinds of strange effects.

Cars, lights, radios, and compasses suddenly stop or react wildly when UFOs pass over. People report strange smells such as ozone, burned matches, or sulfur. And animals react nervously to UFOs. Dogs bark or hide; horses and cows move about anxiously. The lights from UFOs may leave people temporarily sunburned, even after just a brief encounter, and the ground where one lands may be burned. These same effects have been reported over and over again.

In June of 1972 an Iowa soybean field was found with a strange burn mark. Though no one actually saw a UFO land in the field, that seems one possible explanation for the ninety-foot, burned circle.

Unidentified "burn" in Iowa soybean field (courtesy of J. Allen Hynek Center for UFO Studies)

Shapes

The same shapes and sizes of UFOs are reported over and over again. At night people often can't see the shape of a UFO clearly. Sometimes the lights outline the object, but more often the glare keeps the witness from being able to see the shape clearly. One man compared it to trying to see the shape of a car when it comes at you with its headlights on. However, in the daytime people see and report several basic shapes.

For many years, the most commonly described shape was the disk, or "flying saucer." This was a round object, flat toward the edges, thicker in the middle. It was often described as metallic-looking. Sometimes a saucer was reported to have a dome on the top in the center. Some reports mentioned a ring around the outside rim, like the planet Saturn. Sometimes windows were seen. Until about 1963, the "saucer" was the most commonly reported shape, but it has been reported less and less frequently since then.

About one third of the people reporting UFOs describe seeing balls of light, ranging in size from pinpoints to huge fireballs.

About 5% to 8% of UFO witnesses report objects that are cylindrical or cigar-shaped. Other reported shapes include teardrops, metallic balls with "antennas," and doughnuts.

Explanations

Some of these sightings can be explained. For instance, a rare phenomena called ball lightning may account for some balls of fiery light. Unlike the more common jagged streaks of lightning, ball lightning is circular. It travels between five and sixty miles per hour and has been seen to move in many of the strange patterns characteristic of UFOs. It hovers and then takes off very quickly. It changes directions rapidly without slowing down. And it comes to abrupt stops without any gradual slowdown. Ball light-

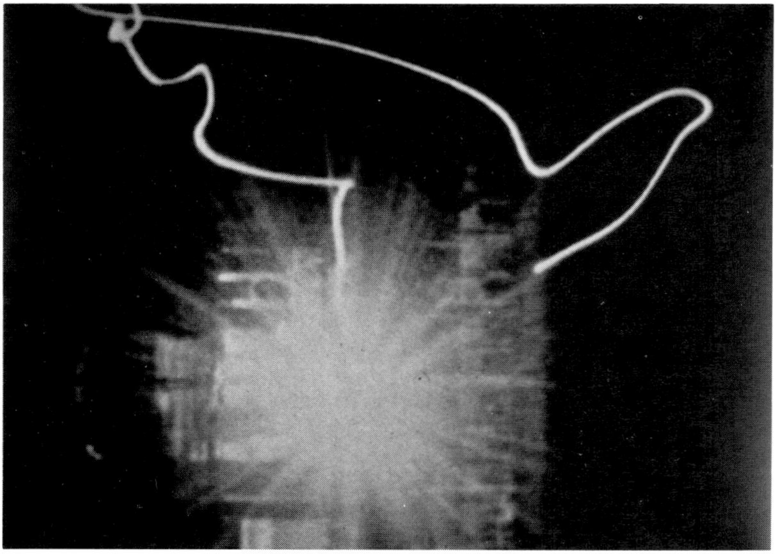

Ball lightning (courtesy of Barry M. King, Parasearch)

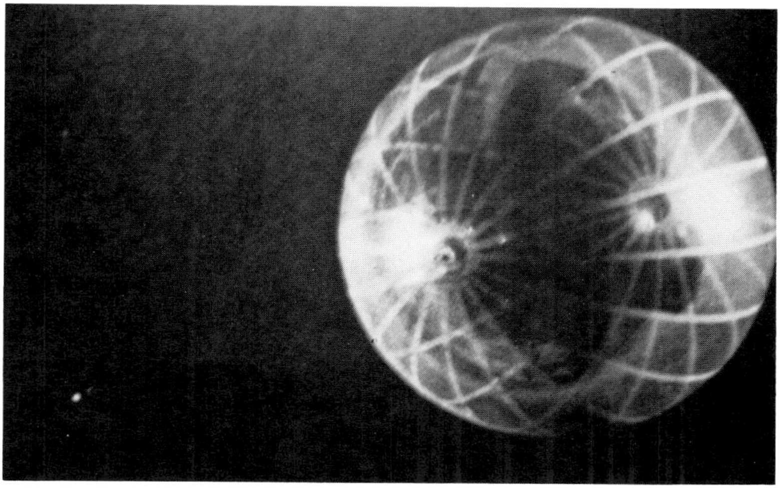

Weather balloon (courtesy of Barry M. King, Parasearch)

ning has been seen to enter homes and move about as if guided by some intelligence, as if it were curious and wanted to explore. Though ball lightning rarely grows bigger than an orange, it has been reported as big as ten feet across. It usually exists for a few minutes and then it evaporates—sometimes quietly, sometimes with a bang!

The planets Venus and Jupiter account for some UFO sightings. At certain times of the year, the light from these planets can be startlingly bright. People get so dazzled by the light from these planets that they think a spaceship is flying through the sky.

Light-colored birds flying at night can look like a formation of spaceships—especially if their bodies reflect moonlight or city lights from below. Even a weather balloon, blown about by the upper wind currents, can look like a spacecraft. Almost anything in the sky, under the right circumstances, can look mysterious enough to be a UFO.

Lenticular clouds, sometimes mistaken for spacecraft (courtesy of Major Ret. Colman S. Vonkeviczky, MMSE, ICUFON)

Possibilities

So what is it that people see when they report a UFO? There are five possibilities: (1) Some people are seeing something natural, such as swamp gas or ball lightning. (2) Some are just imagining they see something strange. (3) Some are deliberately lying, maybe hoping to get on the news. (4) Some might be seeing a man-made object that some government is keeping a secret. (5) And some just might be seeing what UFOs are often claimed to be—alien spacecraft from another planet. Each UFO report has to be investigated individually, and only after the first four are eliminated can the last possibility be considered.

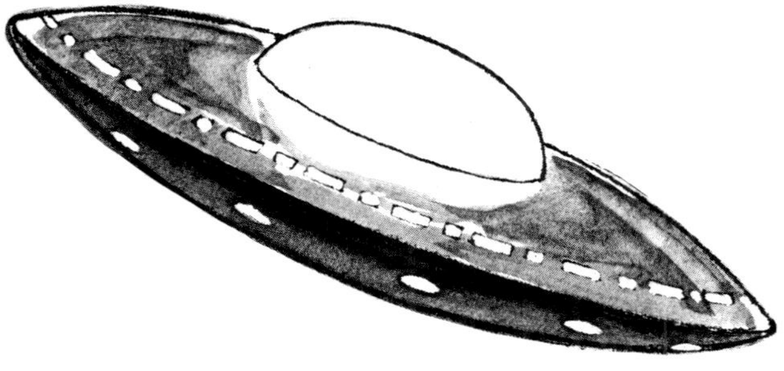

Chapter 3

Close Encounters of the First Kind

Whatever UFOs are, there are thousands of recorded sightings of them. To make it easier to describe and investigate sightings, scientists have defined some categories. Far-away sightings are either "nocturnal lights" (unusual spots of light in the night sky) or "daylight disks" (unusual craft seen in the daytime). Sightings closer than five hundred feet are close encounters of the first, second, third, and fourth kind. The higher the number, the more intense the encounter.

When a UFO comes within a few-hundred feet of one or more witnesses and leaves no physical evidence of itself behind, the sighting is called a close encounter of the first kind. Often these encounters are the easiest to explain. That's because they are frequently some kind of natural phenomenon. But sometimes they are genuine mysteries.

Norman Muscarello

On September 3, 1965, eighteen-year old Norman Muscarello was hitchhiking home after visiting his girlfriend. It was about two o'clock in the morning. He was cutting through an open field, a few miles from his home, when he saw a huge, glowing object in the sky. It seemed to be about eighty or ninety feet in diameter—about as big as a house. He thought it was circular, but it was hard to tell because of the red, glowing lights that seemed to go around the rim of the object. The lights pulsed on and off, and the object wobbled unsteadily and silently through the sky, coming right at him.

Norman was scared. He dove into a ditch. The object backed off and hovered over a house. Norman waited and watched. Finally, the object moved far enough away so that Norman felt it was safe to run to another nearby house. He pounded on the door and screamed. No one answered.

Norman ran to the road. He waved his arms at a passing car, and the car stopped. The people in the car took Norman to the police station in the town of Exeter, New Hampshire.

The police wanted to laugh at Norman's report, but they could see how upset he was. They knew something had happened to him. Norman kept insisting that someone had to go with him to where he'd seen the object.

The station-house police called Officer Eugene Bertrand. He came in and reported that he'd just talked to a woman who was driving in the same area. She was very upset too. She said a huge object with red lights chased her car for twelve miles. Officer Bertrand thought she was a kook. He did, however, agree to take Norman back to where he'd seen "the Thing."

When they got to the field, Norman and Officer Bertrand didn't see anything. Officer Bertrand, who had been in the Air Force, tried to convince Norman that what he saw was a helicopter. They got out of the car to look around. Suddenly, the horses in a nearby corral began to whinny and kick. Dogs began to howl. Norman yelled, "I see it! I see it!"

Officer Bertrand turned, and both he and Norman saw a huge, round object rising from behind some trees. Its red lights were so bright that the nearby white houses looked blood-red. Officer Bertrand started to go for his gun—and then decided perhaps he'd better not. Norman was frozen in his spot, so Officer Bertrand grabbed him and pulled him behind the squad car. The object hovered about one hundred feet off the ground, about a football field's distance from the men. It made no noise at all. Its lights went on and off in a pattern from right to left and left to right about every two seconds. Then the object moved.

Officer Bertrand knew of many kinds of aircraft from his service in the Air Force, but he said that he had never seen anything move the way this object did. It darted this way and that, turning abruptly and stopping and starting suddenly.

A second police officer, Patrolman David Hunt, arrived. He watched with Norman and Officer Bertrand as the object moved off, rocking slightly, its lights pulsating.

Over the next several weeks, many UFOs were seen in the Exeter area. They are written about in *Incident at Exeter* by John G. Fuller. Fuller interviewed over sixty people who reported seeing something strange in the skies around Exeter. These were ordinary people who spoke honestly about something that confused and scared them. Many had lived near the Air Force base all their lives and could recognize all the different kinds of aircraft. Many were also trained observers who were not easily excited, such as the two police officers who saw the first UFO that September night.

Lots of people have tried to explain the Exeter sightings. At first, the Air Force insisted that Norman and the police officers had observed an exercise the Air Force planes had done that night. But when they checked the times, they discovered that all the Air Force planes were back on the ground half an hour before Norman saw the object for the first time.

Many other explanations have been offered—an advertising plane, ball lightning, the planet Jupiter. But though each fits logically with some of the reported facts, none fully accounts for everything that was reported.

A bright planet can be mistaken for a spacecraft. (courtesy of NASA)

Foo Fighters

During World War II, military pilots had many close encounters of the first kind. While flying bombing missions over Europe and Japan, pilots reported glowing spheres and disks. These lights played "tag" with the planes. Sometimes they approached planes at high speed and then stopped abruptly. They circled planes or followed after them. Then they suddenly took off.

Pilots named these lights, "foo fighters," from a popular comic strip. Pilots sometimes tried to get away from the foo fighters, but they never succeeded. The foo fighters left when they were ready to leave.

The foo fighters were reported to be as small as one-foot across and as big as five-feet across. They ranged in color from orange to white to red. Foo fighters seen in the daylight were described as metallic. Sometimes several foo fighters followed a plane, flying in formation, but they never did any harm.

Allied pilots thought the foo fighters were some sort of secret weapon, even though they never hurt anyone. They thought they might have been sent by the enemy to make pilots nervous. But after the war was over, it was learned that Japanese and German pilots also saw foo fighters. Even pilots during the Korean and Vietnam wars saw similar UFOs.

Some foo fighters were probably ball lightning or some other natural phenomena, such as ice glistening on the wings. Some were probably a bright planet. But some of the sightings don't fit any natural explanation. Some UFO investigators suggest that foo fighters might have been sent by an alien culture to examine earth's military activities.

Captain Thomas F. Mantell, Jr.

There are many other recorded close encounters of the first kind. In 1948, Captain Thomas F. Mantell, Jr. was the first to die from one. On January 7, the Air National Guard received a report of a UFO from the Kentucky Highway Patrol. They said it was a silvery-white, ice-cream-cone-shaped object. Several fighter planes were in the air and investigated. At 3:15 p.m. Captain Mantell radioed that he could see the object. It was metallic and of tremendous size. He said he was going up for a closer look.

No one knows for sure what happened next. There was no further radio contact with Captain Mantell, and sometime later the wreckage of his plane was found. The official explanation is that Captain Mantell blacked out from lack of oxygen. After he fainted, his plane crashed. The object he chased is supposed to have been a weather balloon.

However, an experienced pilot and captain in the Air National Guard should have been able to recognize a weather balloon and should have known if lack of oxygen was becoming a problem. Also, both Captain Mantell's watch and his airplane's clock were found in the wreckage. They were both stopped at 3:18, just three minutes after his last radio contact. That doesn't seem enough time for him to get into trouble and for the plane to crash.

A frequently reported effect of UFOs is for lights or

Hovering craft photographed over Kanah, Utah, in 1968 (courtesy of Major Ret. Colman S. Vonkeviczky, MMSE, ICUFON)

engines to suddenly stop. Some people believe Captain Mantell came too close to the UFO, and that some force from the UFO caused the clocks and the plane engines to stop. We will probably never know for sure what caused Captain Mantell to crash.

A Bright Planet and a Little Imagination

Many pilots, policemen, astronomers, and other trained observers have reported close encounters of the first kind. They and thousands like them have seen something strange up close. Maybe some of these sightings have been just a bright planet and a little imagination. But many of them have never been explained.

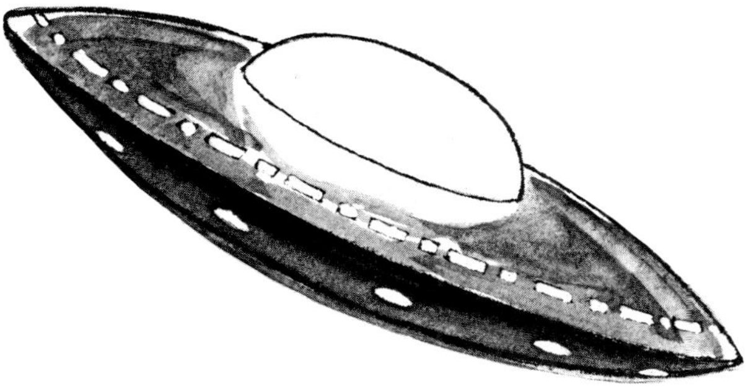

Chapter 4

Close Encounters of the Second Kind

A close encounter of the second kind occurs when a UFO is seen, comes within a few hundred feet, and leaves some kind of physical evidence that it was there. This evidence could be a physical effect on people or machinery, a burn on the ground, a photograph or radar echo, or even a piece of the UFO. Sometimes a UFO will not come close enough to be considered a true "close encounter," but it can still leave physical evidence behind.

There are frequent hoaxes with this kind of encounter. People who say they have seen a UFO usually have really seen something strange. But people who come up with a picture have often faked it. There have been, however, many instances where the evidence has not been faked. These close encounters are genuine mysteries.

Effects on People

In December of 1980, Betty Cash, her friend, Vickie Landrum, and Vickie's grandson, Colby, were driving along a country road in Texas. It was about eight o'clock at night. They saw a fiery object in the sky about five miles ahead. They continued toward it, but stopped about sixty yards from it because it had come down over the road, and Betty was afraid to drive under it. They said it was larger than the car, and they could feel the heat from it.

Betty stood outside the car and watched the UFO for some time. Vickie and Colby came out for a few minutes, but then returned to the car. Eventually the fiery object moved away. Betty, Vickie, and Colby saw what looked like military helicopters "escorting" it.

When they got home, Betty was ill. Her neck, earlobes, and eyelids were swollen. She had blisters on her face. For several days she was unable to see clearly, and a lot of her hair fell out. She suffered vomiting, diarrhea, and headaches. Vickie and Colby had the same symptoms, but they weren't as severe. Perhaps this is because Vickie and Colby stayed in the car for all but a few minutes.

The military denied that they had any aircraft like the one Betty Cash described. They also denied having any helicopters in that area that day. But Betty's symptoms are tangible physical evidence that something was there.

Mechanical Effects

Not only people but also machines can be affected by UFOs. In 1967 Carl Farlow had dramatic evidence of this.

Farlow was driving his diesel truck down a highway in

England between one and two o'clock in the morning. Suddenly, his headlights faded. He pulled over to the side of the road to try to find out what was wrong. Then he saw a large, egg-shaped object flying across the road.

The object was about seventy feet long and about the height of a telephone pole above the ground. It hovered over the road for a few moments, and Farlow studied it. It was dark red with a whitish area near the bottom. Carl heard a humming noise like a refrigerator and smelled something like the smell of a drill going through wood. After a short while, the object left.

When it was gone, Carl noticed another car stopped. He spoke to the driver, who had seen the UFO and whose headlights and engine had also both suddenly stopped. There was a phone booth nearby. Its lights weren't working, but the phone was, so they called the police.

When the police got there, they discovered that the surface of the road appeared melted. Eventually, Farlow learned that more than $1000 damage had been done to his truck, and sixty-five yards of the road had to be resurfaced. He never learned what it was that he saw.

Stopped engines and lights are a frequently reported effect of UFOs. So are large burn areas. These are all evidence of a close encounter.

Photographs

You might think a photograph would be the best evidence of all, but it's not. There are thousands of pictures of UFOs. The problem is they usually can't be verified. If a picture is not in focus or doesn't show some background to serve as a reference, it is hard to be sure what the picture really is. Investigators study the original negatives and the pictures carefully. But even careful study doesn't always eliminate the many pictures of models people have taken. Experts also can't always identify the commonplace objects that only look strange because of the angle at which they were photographed.

Still, there are some "classic" UFO pictures that really seem to prove a close encounter has happened.

In 1950, Mr. and Mrs. Paul Trent photographed a silvery disk flying over their Oregon home. Their two pictures are considered classics, because they include various objects on the ground as reference points and a distinct object in the sky. Analysis of light in the picture by Bruce Maccabee, an optical physicist, seems to indicate that the object was very large and very high up in the sky. However,

Trent photograph (courtesy of Major Ret. Colman S. Vonkeviczky, MMSE, ICUFON)

a writer named Robert Sheaffer has pointed out that there are some telephone wires in the original pictures (which are usually cut off when the pictures are put in UFO books) from which a model could have been hung and photographed.

People have also questioned the photographs of Rex Heflin, a county highway department traffic investigator for California. In August of 1965, he snapped three photos of a strange object flying silently over a California road. The object at first moved very slowly. It was circular and hat-shaped, with a silvery surface. Heflin thought it was about thirty feet around and about 150 feet off the ground. He also reported that a beam of light came from the bottom of the craft. When the UFO suddenly speeded

Heflin photograph (courtesy of J. Allen Hynek Center for UFO Studies)

B-57 bomber photograph (courtesy of J. Allen Hynek Center for UFO Studies)

up and took off, Heflin got a photo of the dark, circular smoke ring it left behind. Skeptics again wonder if the photos could be of a model.

One classic UFO photo is definitely not a model. But nobody can say what it is. It was taken by accident.

About 1954 a publicity picture of a B-57 bomber was taken near Edwards Air Force Base in California. When the photo was developed, a strange object was found in the top, right-hand corner.

It was a disk-shaped object with light and dark areas, giving it dimension. It cast no shadow on the ground as the houses and trees did and seemed in sharper focus than the objects on the ground, as if it were much closer to the camera.

No one was ever able to identify the object, but later reproductions of the photo had the UFO scratched or blotted out. And no one could explain how or why that happened either.

All in all UFO photographs are a curious puzzle. They seem a fascinating clue in this great mystery, but they just can't be relied on. Most investigators want something more.

Movies

In 1978 it seemed they did get something more—a movie of a UFO in action! In December of 1978 there were a number of UFO sightings in New Zealand. These UFOs were both tracked on radar and seen by various pilots.

Quentin Fogarty, an Australian television reporter, went to New Zealand to investigate. He wanted to film the spot of an earlier sighting, so he hired cameraman David Crockett, and his wife, Ngaire Crockett, who recorded sound. He also hired a pilot, Captain Bill Startup, and copilot, Robert Guard. He did not know any of these people before he hired them.

The night of December 30, 1978, Fogarty and the others were flying in the area of the previous sighting. About midnight they noticed strange lights. Ground radar confirmed there was something in the sky there that they couldn't identify. For fifty minutes the lights went on and off, as if something was appearing and disappearing. On the ground, the radar images were also going on and off. There were as many as ten and as few as two images during the fifty minutes.

Captain Startup had to land the plane at 1:00 a.m.

Ngaire Crockett refused to get on the plane again, so when they went back up at 2:16 a.m., a friend of Fogarty's, Dennis Grant, took her place.

About three minutes after takeoff, they saw very bright lights to the right of their plane. They got within ten miles of the object. David Crockett took twelve minutes of film before they lost sight of the object. The object had a brightly-lit, round base and what looked like a transparent dome on top. Crockett also photographed a very bright light which changed colors rapidly from white or yellow-white to dim red and orange.

Experts agree that the object in the movie is not a hoax. They also agree it is not a planet, a weather balloon, a military plane, a meteor, or anything else UFOs often turn

out to be. In fact, no one has been able to identify the object in this movie.

Radar Sightings

In the New Zealand sightings radar was able to confirm that Fogarty and the others saw something real. Most of the time, though, radar evidence is not considered very reliable. Birds, balloons, and unusual weather can all look like UFOs on a radar screen. But there have been a few occasions when radar has picked up genuine UFOs. One famous case happened in Washington, D.C.

In July of 1952, eight objects were picked up on three different radar screens. The objects were flying in restricted air space over the White House and the Capitol Building. They would move at 100 to 300 miles per hour and then suddenly speed up to 800 miles per hour. Airline crews reported strange lights in the sky where the radar said the UFOs were. Military planes were sent to see what was up there. However, as the military planes

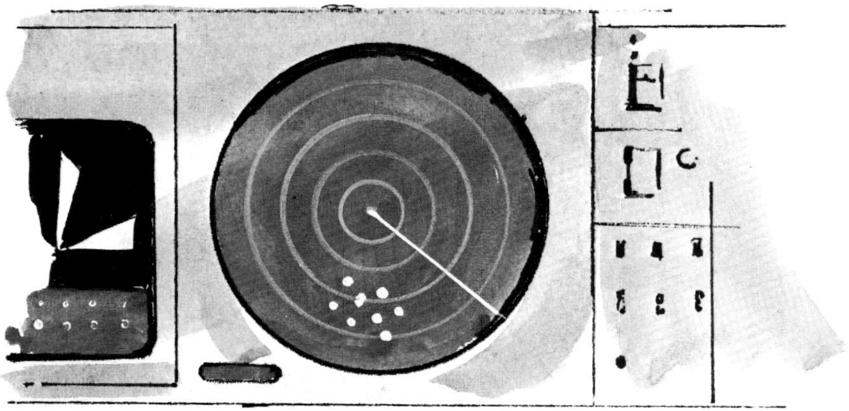

approached, the UFOs disappeared. When the military planes left, the UFOs reappeared. Because these objects were both seen by people and tracked on radar, experts believe there really was something strange that flew over the White House and the Capitol that July evening.

Soil Changes

Experts also believe something strange happened on the Johnson farm in Delphos, Kansas. On November 2, 1971, sixteen-year-old Ronald Johnson saw a strange, glowing object hovering two feet off the ground. After it was gone, the family found a white, glowing circle on the ground where it had been. When they touched the white, crusty substance, their fingers became numb. Later, when it snowed, they discoverd that the snow didn't melt easily over that area.

The soil was analyzed by Dr. Erol A. Faruk, an English chemist. He found that the soil could repel water to a certain degree and that it seemed to have anesthetic qualities. He also found some evidence to confirm the glowing that the Johnsons had reported. But neither he nor any other expert could explain what the white circle was or how it was formed. The experts did agree that no ordinary craft could have caused it.

Bits and Pieces

The experts, however, can't agree on a sighting and explosion that gave scientists actual pieces of a UFO.

In September of 1957, three fishermen watched a flying disk in the sky off the coast of Brazil. Suddenly the disk

"Be sure to clean up everything. We don't want the Earthlings to think we're sloppy."

exploded. Most of the debris was lost in the ocean, but the fishermen did get some pieces of metal.

The metal was analyzed and found to be unusually pure magnesium. That metal would make a good spacecraft because it is very strong. But magnesium that pure was not listed as being made by any company on earth in 1957. People still wonder whether it proves that an alien spacecraft flew over Brazil.

Without a Trace

Considering the number of sightings of UFOs, it seems odd that we have so little physical evidence of them. Some people think that this lack of physical evidence proves that UFOs are all just something natural. Others point out that we do have some evidence that can't be explained. They say maybe we shouldn't expect much evidence. After all, when a person flies from New York to Los Angeles, there is no physical evidence left in any of the states he passes over—but that doesn't mean he wasn't there.

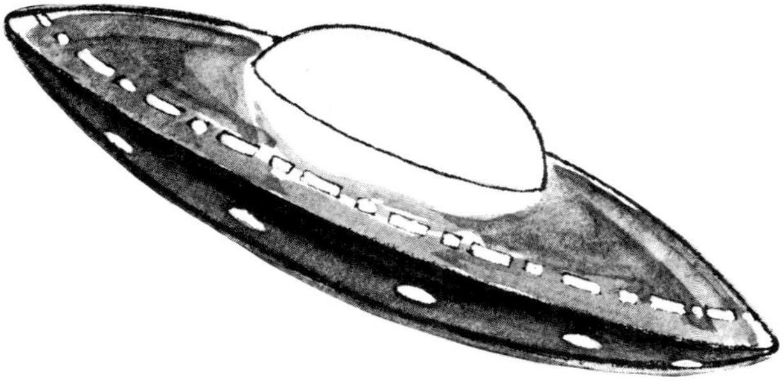

Chapter 5

Close Encounters of the Third Kind

A close encounter of the third kind involves not only seeing a UFO up close, but also seeing occupants in or near that UFO. These sightings are very controversial. Whether or not people believe them depends on whether or not people believe the witnesses are sane, honest people.

Southern France

In 1965 in southern France, a forty-one-year-old farmer went to work in his field about 5:45 one morning. He heard a whistling noise and saw a football-shaped object in the field. It was ten feet to twelve feet long and seven feet tall—about the size of a car. It stood on six legs, had a door, and also had a transparent dome on top. At first the farmer thought it was a strange kind of helicopter, but then he saw the creatures.

Two small figures were near the craft. They were about three feet tall, wearing grey-green clothes. Their heads were huge and bald. They had large ears, lidless eyes, no chins, and round holes for mouths. When they saw the farmer, one pointed a pencil-like object at him. It shot a beam of light at the farmer, and he froze, unable to move, but still able to see.

The creatures quickly got into their craft and flew off. The object made no noise as it left the ground, and it disappeared when it was fifteen yards to twenty yards off the ground. About fifteen minutes later, the farmer found himself once again able to move and go about his business.

This sighting might have been dismissed as imagination, except for two things. The farmer was very highly respected in his community, and the craft left evidence of its visit on the ground. There were deep imprints on the ground from the legs, and, even more mysterious, the soil was changed where the craft had sat. That soil contained 18% calcium, even though the nearby soil contained almost no calcium.

Socorro, New Mexico

The sighting made by the farmer in France could have been a hallucination. The farmer wasn't a trained observer, and he might have made some kind of a mistake about what happened. But officers of the law are trained to observe very carefully. Yet some of them have seen very mysterious things.

At about 5:45 in the evening of April 24, 1964, Deputy

Marshall Lonnie Zamora chased a speeding driver outside Socorro, New Mexico. Before he could catch up to the car, he was distracted by a blue and orange flame in the sky and a loud roar. He knew of a dynamite shack in the area and thought it had blown up.

Zamora radioed the police station to report the explosion and turned off the main road to investigate. As he drove along, he spotted a shiny-white, egg-shaped object in a gully and two figures standing next to it. The figures were human in shape, but they were only about four feet tall. They were wearing white coveralls. Zamora reported that one of the figures looked startled to see his police car approach. At that time Zamora thought the shiny-white object was an overturned car.

The road took Zamora behind a ridge, and for a short time he couldn't see the object or the figures. When he cleared the ridge, the figures were gone. Zamora stopped about one hundred feet from the object. He got out of his car and went toward it. He could see that it was oval and stood on four legs in the gully. On its side was a strange design in red.

Suddenly there was a loud roar. Lonnie hit the dirt, thinking the thing was about to explode. Instead, it rose into the air. It hovered about fifteen feet off the ground, and the roar faded to a whine and then to silence. Then the object flew away.

Sergeant Sam Chavez arrived at the scene, but he was too late to see the object. He and Zamora examined the site where the object had been. They found four indentations in the ground where the object's legs had been, and

SOCORRO, N.M. April 4 1964. At 5:45PM

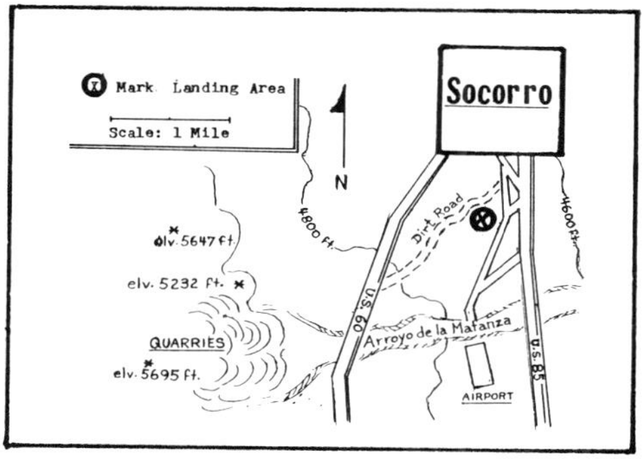

Deputy Marshal Lonnie ZAMORA

1

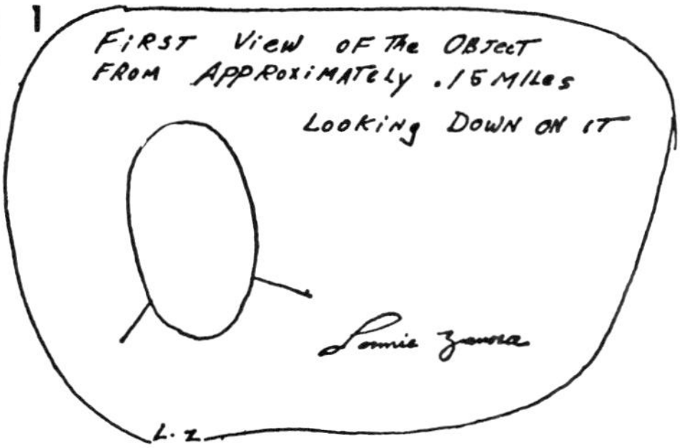

2

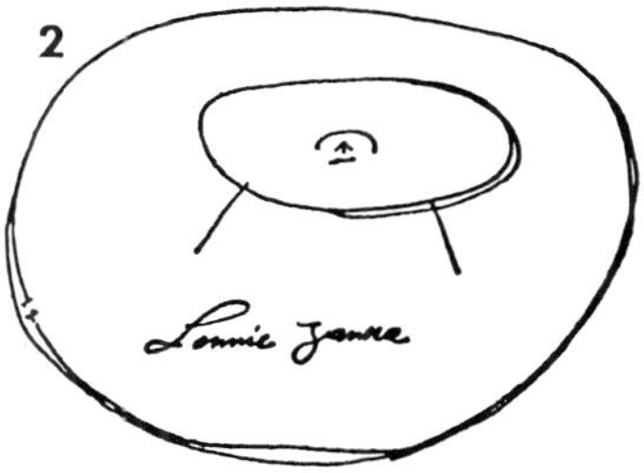

SKETCH OF OBJECT
FROM MY POSITION-
AT APPROXIMATELY 103 FT.-

3

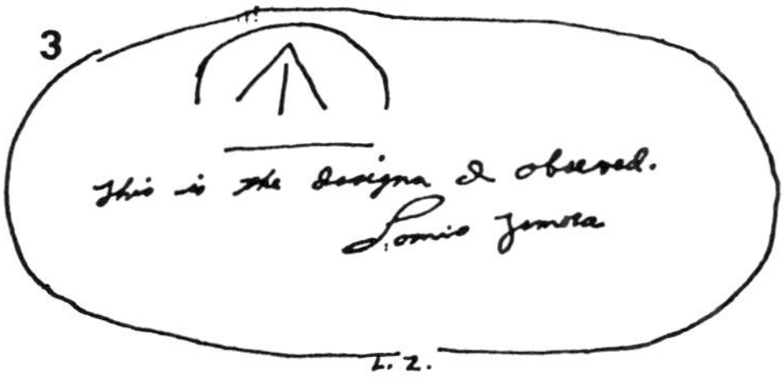

OBSERVED "INSIGNA" LOCATED APPROX-
INATELY AT CENTER OF OBJECT AS SEEN
FROM ABOVE SIDE.

Courtesy of Major Ret. Colman S. Vonkeviczky, MMSE, ICUFON

several bushes which had been burned. They also found what might have been footprints on the hard sand. The footprints had a peculiar hourglass shape.

The Air Force and the FBI investigated this case. They took pictures of the indentations in the sand, the burned bushes, and the footprints, but they couldn't explain what Lonnie Zamora saw. One investigator found some metal scrapings on a rock, but the analysis of it told nothing. Witnesses came forward and said that they saw the object while it was in the sky. Though some have claimed the whole incident was a hoax, officially the sighting remains unexplained.

One of the indentations in the ground found in Socorro, New Mexico (courtesy of Major Ret. Colman S. Vonkeviczky, MMSE, ICUFON)

(courtesy of J. Allen Hynek Center for UFO Studies)

New Guinea

It's hard to believe a law officer with a spotless reputation would deliberately fake a sighting, but it's even harder to believe that a highly-educated Anglican priest would. In 1959 the Reverend William Booth Gill, a missionary in New Guinea, reported a close encounter.

There had been many UFO sightings in New Guinea that year, but in June, Reverend Gill wrote to a friend that he thought UFOs were just some kind of electrical phenomenon. He signed his letter "Doubting William." Then one evening he came out of the dining hall and looked up at the sky. Next to the planet Venus, which he recognized, was a sparkling object. Thirty-seven natives, most of them children in the mission school, joined Reverend Gill and watched as the object came closer. It was a circular craft with a large base and a smaller upper deck. They could see four legs on the base. What was even more amazing was that they could also see four human-like figures on the upper deck. The figures seemed to be working on the craft and would occasionally go inside and then return outside. The craft was like nothing any of them had ever seen before.

For several hours, all thirty-eight people watched the craft. Three more small ships appeared, and a larger "mother ship" hovered high in the sky. Then at about 10:50, the UFOs disappeared.

The next evening, the ships appeared again. Again a crowd gathered to watch. This time the mother ship came down low. Gill waved to an occupant that seemed to be looking at him. To his surprise, the figure waved back. A native waved two arms, and two figures on the craft raised their arms. As darkness fell, Gill signaled with a flashlight, and the ship rocked in acknowledgment. However, after this, the figures ignored the people on the ground. Soon after, they left.

On the third night, Reverend Gill reported eight ships in the sky, but only one came low and no figures were seen. After that night, the ships did not reappear in that location.

Twenty-five of the witnesses to this event signed statements describing what they saw. And within a one-year period, over sixty more sightings were made in New Guinea. Some skeptics still claim that Reverend Gill and the others just saw bright planets or that they made up the whole thing. Some think it is one of the most convincing

"Why do we always have to come to Earth for our vacations?"

stories on record. When Reverend Gill wrote of the incident to his friend, he signed the letter "Believing Bill."

Alien Visitors?

There are many stories of people seeing not just strange objects in the sky, but also strange creatures who seem to pilot those crafts. Some of the creatures are short and bald with large heads and large eyes; others are more like humans. Perhaps the people who see "aliens" are mistaken in what they see, or perhaps they have deliberately made up the whole thing. Maybe there are no close encounters of the third kind—but maybe there are!

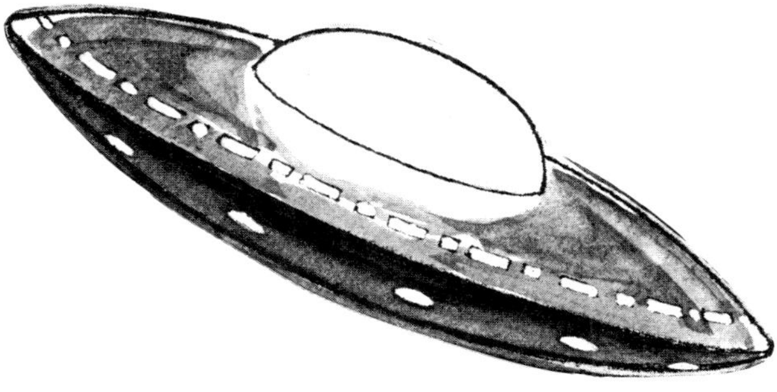

Chapter 6

Close Encounters of the Fourth Kind

Just seeing alien creatures would be frightening, but what if it went further? What if it became a close encounter of the fourth kind—an abduction! That's what more and more people are starting to report has happened to them.

Betty and Barney Hill

One of the first reported abductions happened in September of 1961 to Betty and Barney Hill. Their story is told in *The Interrupted Journey* by John G. Fuller. Late one night Betty and Barney Hill were driving home. They had been on vacation in Canada and were headed to New Hampshire. Betty noticed a bright light in the sky moving about strangely. It seemed to follow them. They stopped the car and studied it through a pair of binoculars. Barney insisted that it had to be an airplane. Betty insisted it couldn't be.

The object was cigar-shaped and had flashing red, green, and blue lights. The Hills couldn't hear any noise coming from it. They puzzled about it, but finally got back in the car and drove on. The object continued to follow them.

The Hills drove on for a while. Then Betty insisted they stop again and get out to look at the object. Barney didn't want to, but he did. Barney still denied it was anything unusual.

This time when they stopped, the object flew over the road about fifty feet above the Hills. Both Barney and Betty saw windows in the object and at least six figures in uniforms at the windows. Barney, without knowing why, followed the object into a nearby field. Betty screamed for him to come back. Barney saw the craft land and the figures come out of the craft. He knew that he shouldn't go toward the craft, but he felt as if he was in some kind of trance. Then, suddenly, he remembered he had the binoculars on a strap around his neck. He grabbed them and pulled, ripping the strap across the back of his neck. This brought him back to himself, and he raced back to the car. He and Betty drove off in a panic.

The next thing he and Betty remember, they were thirty-five miles down the road. Later, in discussing the incident with others, they realized that they got home about two hours later than they had expected to. Their watches had both stopped running and the tops of Barney's shoes were badly scuffed.

Though the Hills reported the incident, they did not dwell on it. Betty did have dreams about aliens abducting them, but dismissed them as just dreams. Barney had trouble with high blood pressure and ulcers and consulted a psychiatrist. He thought his problems came from the stress of his job.

A few years passed. The psychiatrist had been able to help Barney some, but he felt hypnosis might be helpful in uncovering what was bothering Barney so much. Both Barney and Betty underwent hypnosis, and, without knowing what the other said, each told the same strange story.

It went like this: after Barney and Betty drove off, the aliens stopped their car. Both Barney and Betty were taken into the spacecraft. Barney was dragged, scuffing the tops of his shoes. They were given thorough medical exams in separate rooms. Then they were released and sent on their way with instructions to forget what had happened.

Investigators do not know what to think about this incident. Skeptics do not think the Hills are deliberately lying, but they do think Betty might have unintentionally planted the story in Barney's mind when she told him her dreams. Whatever happened that night clearly frightened both of them—and it seems to have happened to a lot of other people since then.

Travis Walton

In November of 1975 seven young men were returning from a day of chopping trees in Sitgreaves National Forest in Arizona. Attracted by a strange glow in a nearby clearing, they stopped and found a circular object hovering about fifteen feet off the ground. It was about fifteen or twenty feet in diameter, about eight feet tall, and had a dome on the top.

One of the men, named Travis Walton, got out of the truck to take a closer look. He approached to within a few feet of the object. Then, suddenly, he was hit by a beam of light from it. He fell to the ground unconscious. The others drove off in a panic, but didn't go far. They returned about twenty minutes later to look for Travis. They couldn't find him or the object.

They returned to town scared and contacted the police. The police were convinced the men had murdered Travis and had made up a crazy story to cover it up. Over the next two days they conducted a massive search for Travis. Fifty trained men searched the entire area. They couldn't find him. After two full days they gave up, thinking even if he had been alive, he could not have survived the freezing cold nights.

Five days after the sighting, Travis called his family from a phone booth twelve miles from the abduction site. He thought he had only been gone for about an hour and a half. He had five days' growth of beard, was very thirsty but not hungry, and showed no signs of exposure, even though the temperature had been below freezing each night he had been missing.

Travis reported that he had awakened on a table inside an alien spacecraft. The craft seemed to be in space. Travis described the creatures on board as about five feet tall with large bald heads and large eyes. They had white, marshmallowy skin. When the aliens left him alone, Travis was able to look around the ship, but nothing made any sense to him.

Then the object landed in a sort of hangar. Travis didn't have any idea where the hangar was. A human took Travis from the spacecraft into the hangar where several disk-shaped crafts were parked. The human did not speak to him. Travis also saw three other human beings there. All were wearing helmets. He tried to communicate with them, but an object like an oxygen mask was placed over

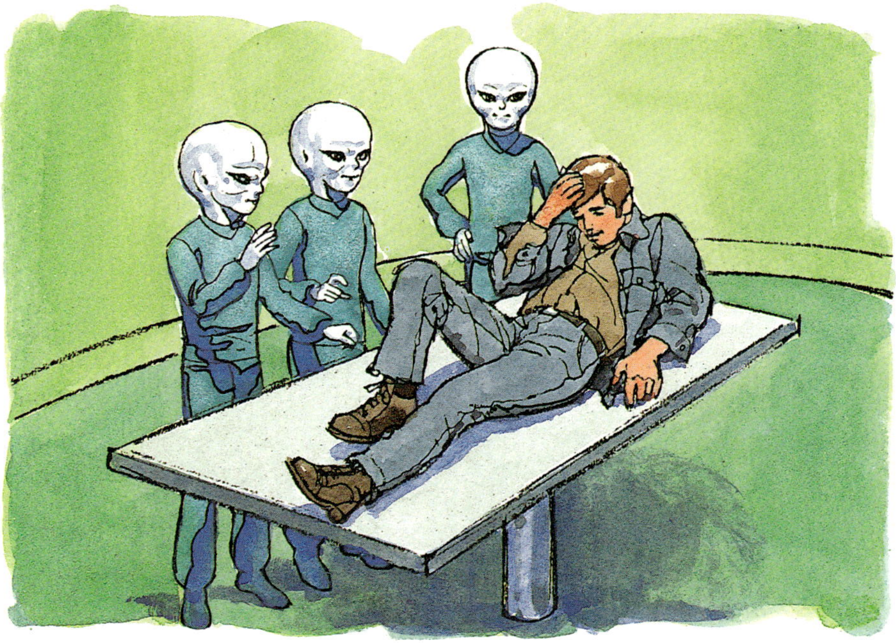

his face, and he passed out. When he awoke, he was on the road, near the phone booth from which he called his family.

All but one of the six witnesses to this incident passed a lie-detector test, as did Travis himself. (Travis did not pass the first lie-detector test he took, which was given very soon after he returned. He said he was still too upset over the incident for the test to be valid. He was given another test several months after the incident, which he passed easily.) All seven men had trouble putting their lives in

order after this experience. Yet some skeptics claim this whole story is a deliberate lie. Travis tells his version of the story in *The Walton Experience.*

Being abducted once would be scary enough, but some people claim they have been abducted over and over again.

Whitley Strieber

In 1986 Whitley Strieber, a best-selling author of horror stories, began experiencing great uneasiness. He became easily confused, unable to work, and was often tired. He had a hard time getting along with his wife and young son. Parts of his body hurt, and he had cuts and scabs in places he couldn't remember having injured. He did have a vivid memory of having seen a large owl one night, but part of him was aware that he hadn't really seen any such animal. He was afraid to remember what he had really seen.

Then memories began popping into his mind. Memories of small figures coming into his bedroom at night —memories of them taking him, talking to him, and examining him. Strieber underwent hypnosis and suddenly, a whole series of stories came out. Under hypnosis, Strieber described being first abducted when he was twelve years old and being taken over and over again ever since then by small alien creatures.

The creatures were about three feet tall, with bald heads and big slanted eyes. Strieber never knew why they kept examining him, but they seemed to be doing some kind of experiment on him.

Strieber tells his story in his book, *Communion.* In it he admits he himself doesn't know if these abductions really happened or if they just happened in his mind. He says his memories of these events do not feel any different from his memories of other past events. He remembers not only what happened, but also what the creatures sounded like, how they smelled, and how they felt. There is also the physical evidence of the cuts and sore spots and personality changes.

Even more convincing is the fact that other people also claim to have seen strange things while visiting Strieber's house. They report strange lights, noises, and other disturbances on the nights Strieber remembers under hypnosis as nights he was taken. Strieber's son was told nothing about the aliens. Yet when he was asked about any unusual dreams, he described some little creatures who came at night and examined him. And he also remembered strange lights and noises.

Strieber's wife also seemed to be aware that something was going on. When she underwent hypnosis, she spoke of her husband's frequent absences from bed in the middle of the night. At first she said that he was up writing or that he was checking on their son. But then she said, "They come for Whitley, and he's supposed to go. But I'm not supposed to go." When asked, "Who came?", she said, "Nobody that I know of." Later she said she knew she couldn't stop them and that her role was to help Strieber feel normal and secure after he came back.

To most people, these stories probably sound crazy. Even Strieber worries that he might be mentally ill. But the

psychiatrists and psychologists who have tested him all say he's completely sane and normal.

Budd Hopkins, a noted UFO researcher, has reported many stories similar to Strieber's in his books, *Missing Time* and *Intruders*. He has found that many of the people who have come to him with these stories have similar scars on the back of a leg. These people sometimes remember that they found themselves bleeding one day, sometimes enough to require stitches, and yet they don't know how they cut themselves. Under hypnosis, they all tell stories similar to Strieber's.

Overactive Imaginations?

Most people dismiss stories of close encounters of the fourth kind as either outright lies or the product of overactive imaginations. Hypnosis can help people remember events they've blocked from their minds, but sometimes people say things they think the questioner wants to hear, and then they start to believe the stories are really true. The people who tell these stories all say they really believe something happened to them. And maybe it did!

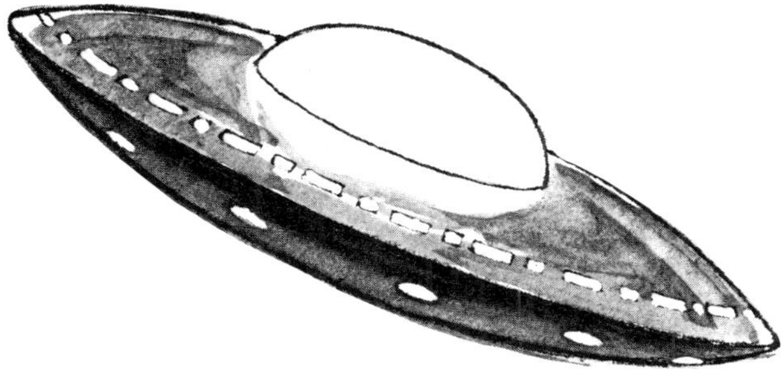

Chapter 7
Investigating UFOs

Many people are seeing strange things in the sky. They claim to have seen spacecraft and aliens. They even claim that the aliens sometimes abduct people. What's being done about it? Who is trying to find out what, if anything, is really happening?

Project Sign

In the United States, the first investigation into UFOs was done by the government, who assigned the investigation to the Air Force. However, right from the start, the government seemed more interested in proving that there were no such things as UFOs than in finding out the truth about what people were seeing. The investigation began in 1947 and was called, at first, Project Sign. In its first year Project Sign found it couldn't explain 20% of the UFO sightings it investigated. It turned in a final report on them, which some people say concluded that the sightings it couldn't explain were alien spacecraft.

Some people claim that when the Chief of Staff read Project Sign's report, he was so angry he burned the report. We don't know what the report said, but we do know that many of the investigators were fired, and Project Sign was replaced by Project Grudge. Investigators for Project Grudge have said that they were told to explain everything. From this point on, the official government position has been that the idea of UFOs is ridiculous and people who believe in them are either misled or crazy.

Project Grudge

In its first year Project Grudge found it couldn't explain 23% of its cases. So Project Grudge decided the sightings it couldn't explain were just people's imaginations. The investigation slowed down, and UFOs were ignored for a while. Then, in 1951, Captain Edward J. Ruppelt was placed in charge of the project. He put new energy into the program, and, in 1952, the investigation was upgraded and given a new name: Project Blue Book.

The Robertson Panel

In 1953, the CIA entered the UFO investigation. In response to the public demand for an answer to the UFO question, it formed a committee of top scientists from all over the country. The committee was called the Robertson Panel. The Robertson Panel was concerned that

UFOs might represent a threat to our country's security. They studied the issue and decided that UFOs themselves were not a threat, but UFO reports were. The CIA was afraid that if an enemy attacked our country, the report might be ignored as just another UFO sighting until it was too late. The CIA thought it would be best if people stopped reporting UFOs. They used the panel of scientists to stress sightings that had simple explanations and to ridicule people who thought UFOs were real. They also started a public relations campaign to convince Americans that genuine UFOs do not exist.

Project Blue Book

The report of the Robertson Panel influenced the attitude at Project Blue Book. Their focus switched from a serious investigation to simply trying to prove that UFOs

UFO investigators (courtesy of Barry M. King, Parasearch)

"I don't care how many reports we can't explain! There are no such things as UFOs!"

were ordinary things that were being misunderstood. Project Blue Book refused to release any information about a sighting unless it had been explained—and any military personnel who did release other information could be fined up to $10,000 and be sentenced to up to ten years in jail.

But despite the government's attitude and the ridicule in the press, a poll showed that more people believed UFOs were real than did not. Some scientists also came forward and said the problem should again be studied seriously. They pressured the government to really do something.

The Condon Committee

In 1966 the government formed the Condon Committee to investigate UFOs. It contained top scientists and worked out of the University of Colorado. Its purpose was to find out what UFOs are or, at least, to find out if they were worth further study.

Believers in UFOs were encouraged, but, before the committee even began its work, it was clear that the leaders of the committee weren't taking their job seriously. Dr. Edward Condon, the head of the committee, openly said, before they even started, that he didn't think the government should bother studying UFOs. He was sure that there wasn't anything to them.

The committee studied UFOs for two years. They found that they couldn't explain 22% of the cases they investigated—and this was not due to lack of information, but rather to genuinely mysterious encounters. Nevertheless

Dr. Condon concluded in the final report that there was nothing at all in UFO reports. He recommended that the government stop investigating them.

Some members of the Condon Committee strongly disagreed with Dr. Condon's conclusions and published their own report. They pointed to the 22% of the sightings that were genuine unknowns and said that UFOs deserved further study. But the press just published Dr. Condon's conclusions, and the government closed Project Blue Book. The U.S. government was officially out of the business of investigating UFOs.

Private Organizations

Citizen groups then began to try to investigate UFOs on their own—and did so with more open minds. One of the most important groups was founded by Dr. J. Allen Hynek, an astronomer who had been a consultant to Project Blue Book. Dr. Hynek had begun his investigations not believing UFOs were real. However, as he studied actual sightings and talked with witnesses, he became convinced something real was happening. He formed the Center for UFO Studies (CUFOS), which began gathering facts and publishing reports.

APRO (Aerial Phenomena Research Organization), NICAP (National Investigations Committee on Aerial Phenomena), and MUFON (Mutual UFO Network) were already working on the mystery. These groups worked seriously on the problem. Unfortunately, some "kook" groups were also formed—and they tended to get most of the publicity.

Unidentified craft (courtesy of Barry M. King, Parasearch)

As the serious groups worked, many of them began to suspect that the U.S. government was not out of the business of investigating UFOs and that the U.S. government knew more about UFOs than it was telling the public.

Private UFO investigators reported that their phones were tapped and that they received threats not to talk about certain UFO sightings. These threats seemed to come from U.S. military officers. Investigators tried to get records from Project Blue Book files. They asked for the records on different sightings and investigations, only to be told that those records were still classified Top Secret. People could only wonder: if UFOs are not real, why should the sighting reports and investigation details remain top secret?

Then Air Force employees began coming forward. They said the government actually had alien spacecraft and that the bodies of alien creatures were hidden away in different military bases.

Roswell, New Mexico

One of the most famous rumors of a crashed alien spacecraft began in 1947. On July 2, near Roswell, New Mexico, people reported seeing bright lights moving strangely about the sky. Then a rancher named W. W. Brazel contacted the Air Force. He reported that something unusual had exploded near his ranch and that he had found some of the remains.

The Air Force sent intelligence officers to collect whatever it was that Brazel had found. Witnesses who saw the debris described several different types of material.There were beams that looked like wood, covered with strange figures that may have been writing. These beams were very light-weight, yet could not be bent or burned. There were also pieces of metal, which were extremely strong, and brown pieces of parchment-like substances, which also had strange figures on them. There was enough debris to fill a truck, but the main body of the craft didn't seem to be there. Had it crashed somewhere else? Some people think so.

A man named Barney Barnett claimed he and a group of students from an eastern university saw a crashed object in the desert west of Roswell. It was metallic and disk-shaped. Barnett said they also saw dead bodies near the craft. They were about four feet tall with round, bald heads that seemed too large for their bodies. He and the students studied the wreck for only a few minutes before military officers arrived and told them to leave and say nothing about what they had seen.

The local Air Force public-relations officer issued a press release saying that the Air Force had a crashed UFO disk in its possession. Later, he was reprimanded for issuing such a statement, and the Air Force told the press that the debris on Brazel's ranch was from a crashed weather balloon.

Many people saw the actual debris from the ranch. They state firmly that whatever it was from, it was not from a crashed weather balloon, which is made from very flimsy material. Military personnel that handled the debris say the Air Force substituted a real weather balloon for the actual debris when talking to the press. We will probably never know for sure what the Air Force collected from the ranch and the desert, but rumors persist that what they really found was a crashed alien spacecraft and crew.

Other Reports

There are many such stories, fueled by statements from people who worked for the military. All of them claim they actually saw alien spacecraft and alien creatures at top secret bases. And all of them say the military ordered them not to talk about it.

Raymond E. Fowler, in *Casebook of a UFO Investigator,* tells of an engineer who worked for the Air Force in 1953. The engineer claims that on May 20, 1953, he was taken by the military in a plane and then on a bus to an unknown spot. The windows on the bus were covered and everyone on the bus was told they were going to investigate the crash of a super-secret Air Force vehicle.

They weren't supposed to talk to each other or do anything other than their jobs.

The engineer described the crashed vehicle as oval-shaped. He said it looked like "two deep saucers" stacked one upside down on top of the other. It was a dull silver color and had a door which opened from the top down forming a ramp. The engineer's job was to determine how fast the vehicle was going when it crashed.

Disregarding his orders, the engineer peeked into a nearby tent. He saw the dead bodies of four-foot-tall,

human-like creatures. For twenty years he did not tell anyone—and with good reason. Before everyone boarded the bus for the ride home, they had to take an oath not to tell anyone what they had seen.

Many other people have also come forward, describing what they claim is hidden on various military bases. One woman, dying of cancer, came forward, telling how she had cataloged hundreds of items from a recovered UFO. She also claimed to have seen alien bodies, four to five feet tall, with large heads and slanted eyes. She said she decided to tell her story, because, "Uncle Sam can't do anything to me once I'm in my grave."

Why a Secret?

Why would the government try to keep such things secret? Why would it claim UFOs aren't real, and then secretly investigate them? Why would it threaten investigators, telling them not to talk about sightings?

Most people think the government hopes to learn amazing secrets from aliens and doesn't want any other government to find out. Others think the government is afraid people will panic if they know the truth. Citizen UFO groups think the secrecy does more harm than good. They are working to get the information out into the open.

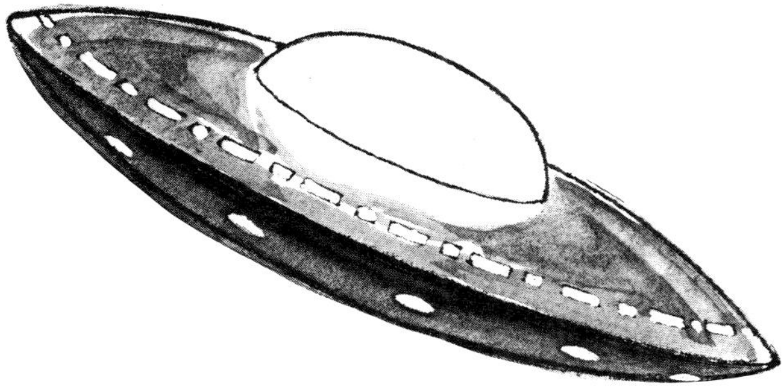

Chapter 8

UFOs Today

Still With Us

On November 17, 1986 Kenju Terauchi, a Japanese pilot with nineteen years experience, reported a huge object, followed by two smaller objects, keeping pace with the 747 cargo jet he was piloting over the Alaskan wilderness. Terauchi said the object was walnut-shaped, and that it showed up on his on-board weather radar. Both the Anchorage air-traffic controllers and the U.S. Air Force also had blips on their radar screens for a moment, but lost them. The object stayed with the 747 about half an hour and then disappeared.

Officially, the sighting was dismissed as the planet Jupiter, and the three different radar readings were dismissed as mistakes. In forty years of investigating UFOs we haven't come very far.

Yet, people are as interested in UFOs now as ever before. Tom Weber of Chippewa Falls, Wisconsin, wants to build a landing site for UFOs in Elmwood, Wisconsin. He thinks aliens are only waiting for a friendly invitation from the people of earth before landing openly. Most people are more curious than frightened about the occupants of UFOs. After all, if they've really been visiting us for years, they have never really hurt anyone. People who say they have been abducted are scared, but not physically hurt. (We think.)

Why Visit Earth?

Many people wonder why aliens might come to earth. The most likely reason is to study us. Whitley Strieber reported that the aliens who abducted him told him that the earth is a school. People on earth study all forms of life that live on earth, and even some that died millions of years ago. Why shouldn't aliens study us?

Others suggest that aliens may want something from us. They may need food, or energy sources, or some kind of knowledge. Some think the aliens fear us and might be trying to learn how to defend themselves against our aggression and independence.

People often ask why the aliens (if there are aliens) don't just land and introduce themselves. Strieber again says the aliens told him that they're giving us time to slowy get used to the idea of another life form, so that it isn't such a shock to our culture. Experts point out that we really shouldn't expect truly alien creatures to have the same motives as human beings.

What Are They Really?

UFOs might be just a combination of natural phenomena and imagination, but the evidence needs to be more seriously studied. Too many believable people have seen strange things that remain unexplained.

In 1968, scientists studied eyewitness reports of one of the first satellite re-entries to the earth's atmosphere. They thought this spectacular and unusual sight surely would be mistaken for a UFO. But, in fact, the hundreds of witnesses interviewed were surprisingly accurate in describing what they saw, though most didn't know what it was. People made some mistakes describing its height, size, and speed, but most were very close. No one reported that their car engine and lights failed. No one claimed that it bathed them in radiation or burned their skin. No one thought they had seen occupants in some kind of strange craft.

A Great Mystery

Most scientists agree that there must be life on planets out in the universe somewhere. But they also agree that there probably isn't any life on any of the other planets in our solar system. The nearest star that scientists think could have planets with life is Alpha Centauri. But the fastest craft we have would need 80,000 years to get there.

This makes it sound impossible for craft from another planet to come to earth. But remember—a hundred years ago, most people believed it was impossible to go to the moon. There may be civilizations out in the galaxy who are very far ahead of us. They could be sending spaceships to visit us, using forces we've never heard of.

No one today can say for sure what UFOs are. But we can hope that someday people will solve this Great Mystery.

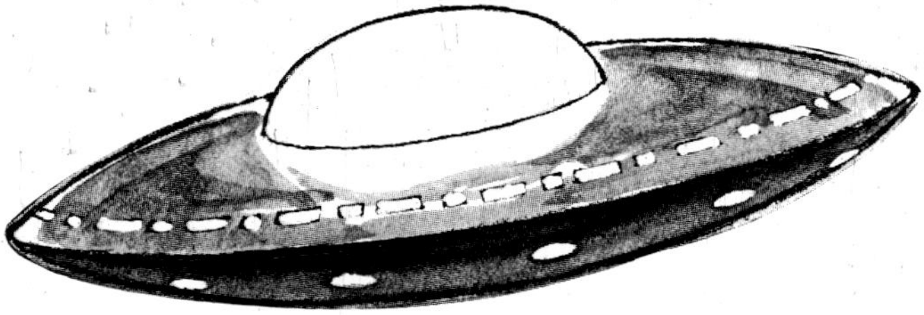

INDEX